Puppy Love 101

A Beginner's Guide to Dog Breeding

"Puppy Love 101: A Beginner's Guide to Dog Breeding" is a comprehensive and informative manual that equips aspiring breeders with the knowledge and guidance they need to navigate the world of dog breeding responsibly, ensuring the health, well-being, and happiness of their furry companions.

TABLE OF CONTENTS

Puppy Love 101

Introduction:

Welcome to "**Puppy Love 101: A Beginner's Guide to Dog Breeding.**" If you've ever dreamed of bringing new life into the world and making a positive impact on the canine community, this guide is here to help you navigate the exciting and rewarding journey of dog breeding.

Breeding dogs is a fulfilling endeavor that requires knowledge, dedication, and a deep love for our four-legged friends. Whether you're a first-time breeder or someone looking to expand their understanding of the breeding process, this guide will provide you with the essential information and guidance you need to get started on the right paw.

Within the pages of this guide, you'll explore the fundamental aspects of dog breeding, from understanding the basics and choosing the right breeds to preparing for breeding, caring for the expectant mother, and nurturing the newborn puppies. We'll delve into topics such as health evaluations, genetics, mating, pregnancy, whelping, early puppy development, nutrition, veterinary care, and responsible placement of the puppies.

Throughout this journey, remember that responsible dog breeding is a commitment to the welfare of the dogs and the betterment of the breed. It requires patience, attention to detail, and a lifelong dedication to the well-being of the puppies you bring into the world.

So, let's embark on this adventure together. Whether your goal is to preserve and improve a specific breed or simply experience the joy of raising a litter of puppies, "Puppy Love 101: A Beginner's Guide to Dog Breeding" is here to provide you with the knowledge and support you need to embark on this beautiful journey of bringing new life into the world of dogs.

Puppy Love 101

Chapter 1: Understanding the Basics: Why Breed Dogs?

Introduction:
Welcome to the exciting world of dog breeding! In this chapter, we'll delve into the fundamental question: Why breed dogs? Whether you have a deep passion for a specific breed or you're simply interested in contributing to the canine community, understanding the reasons behind dog breeding is essential before embarking on this rewarding journey.

1.1 Preserving Breeds:
One significant reason people choose to breed dogs is to preserve and perpetuate specific breeds. Breeding ensures that unique breed traits, characteristics, and temperaments are passed down to future generations. By responsibly breeding, enthusiasts help maintain breed standards, ensuring their beloved breeds continue to thrive.

1.2 Improving Breed Health:
Another motivation for breeding is to improve the overall health of specific breeds. Ethical breeders focus on producing puppies with sound genetic health by carefully selecting breeding pairs with no hereditary health issues. Through responsible breeding practices, genetic diseases can be minimized, leading to healthier and more resilient dogs.

Puppy Love 101

1.3 Working Dogs and Performance Breeding:
Breeding dogs with exceptional working abilities or specific talents is another important aspect of dog breeding. Certain breeds excel in various tasks, such as herding, tracking, or search and rescue. By thoughtfully selecting breeding pairs with proven working abilities, breeders contribute to the development of highly skilled and reliable working dogs.

1.4 Preservation of Rare Breeds:
Some breeds face the risk of becoming endangered or extinct due to declining population numbers. Breeding enthusiasts play a crucial role in preserving these rare breeds by carefully managing their reproduction. By raising awareness, promoting breed recognition, and responsibly breeding rare dogs, enthusiasts help safeguard their existence for future generations to enjoy.

1.5 Responsible Ownership and Education:
Dog breeding can also be a means to promote responsible dog ownership and educate prospective owners. Responsible breeders prioritize the well-being of their dogs, ensuring they go to loving and suitable homes. They provide guidance and support to new owners, educating them about breed-specific needs, training, and responsible pet care.

1.6 Emotional Connection and Fulfillment:
For many breeders, the emotional connection and fulfillment derived from raising and caring for dogs are powerful motivations. The process of witnessing the birth and growth of puppies, the joy of finding them loving homes, and the satisfaction of positively impacting the lives of both dogs and their owners are immeasurable rewards that come with dog breeding.
Conclusion:
Understanding the various motivations behind dog breeding is essential for anyone considering entering this field. Whether it's preserving breed standards, improving health, developing working abilities, preserving rare breeds, promoting responsible ownership, or finding personal fulfillment, dog breeding offers a rich and meaningful experience for passionate individuals dedicated to the well-being and future of our canine companions.

Puppy Love 101

Chapter 2: Choosing the Right Breeds: Finding Your Furry Match

Introduction:
Selecting the right breeds to work with is a crucial decision in dog breeding. The choice of breeds will shape your breeding program, influence the traits of the puppies you produce, and determine the satisfaction and success you experience as a breeder. In this chapter, we'll explore the factors to consider when choosing breeds and provide guidance to help you find your perfect furry match.

2.1 Researching Breeds:
Start by conducting thorough research on different breeds. Consider their characteristics, temperament, exercise requirements, grooming needs, and any breed-specific health issues. Learn about their history, purpose, and any unique considerations involved in breeding them. Understanding the traits and specific requirements of various breeds will help you make informed decisions.

2.2 Assessing Your Goals and Resources:
Reflect on your goals as a breeder. Are you aiming to preserve a particular breed, produce working dogs, or focus on companion animals? Consider your available resources, including time, space, and financial commitments.

Different breeds have varying demands, so choose breeds that align with your goals and resources.

2.3 Understanding Compatibility:

Evaluate the compatibility between yourself and the breeds you're considering. Assess your lifestyle, energy level, and experience as a dog owner. Some breeds thrive in active households, while others prefer a more relaxed environment. Be honest about your capabilities and select breeds that complement your lifestyle.

2.4 Considering Health and Genetics:

Health should be a priority when selecting breeds. Research breed-specific health issues and genetic conditions associated with the breeds you're interested in. Aim to work with breeds that have responsible breeding practices in place, with an emphasis on health testing, genetic screenings, and breed improvement programs.

2.5 Networking and Mentorship:

Connect with experienced breeders, attend dog shows, and join breed-specific clubs or organizations. Networking with knowledgeable individuals can provide valuable insights and guidance in choosing breeds. Seek mentorship from established breeders who can share their expertise and support your journey.

2.6 Evaluating Breeding Lines:

Examine the breeding lines of the breeds you're considering.

Study pedigrees, performance records, and health certifications of potential breeding dogs. Look for dogs that possess the desired traits, temperament, and genetic diversity that align with your breeding goals. Evaluating the lineage will help you make informed decisions and avoid potential issues.

2.7 Considering Demand and Market Trends:

Assess the demand for the breeds you're interested in breeding. Research market trends, popularity, and the availability of potential homes for the puppies you'll produce. While it's essential to breed for the love of the breed itself, understanding market dynamics can help ensure your breeding endeavours are sustainable.

Conclusion:

Choosing the right breeds is a critical foundation for a successful and fulfilling breeding journey. By conducting thorough research, assessing your goals and resources, considering compatibility, prioritizing health and genetics, seeking mentorship, and evaluating breeding lines and market demand, you'll be well-equipped to find your furry match. Remember, each breed has its unique qualities, so take your time to make an informed decision that aligns with your passion and objectives as a responsible breeder.

Puppy Love 101

Chapter 3: Preparing for Breeding: Health, Genetics, and Screening

Introduction:
Before embarking on the journey of breeding dogs, it is crucial to lay a strong foundation by prioritizing the health, genetics, and screening processes. This chapter will guide you through the essential steps to ensure responsible breeding practices and improve the overall quality of the puppies you produce. By taking proactive measures, you'll promote the well-being of both the parent dogs and their offspring.

3.1 Health Evaluations:
Start by conducting comprehensive health evaluations on both potential parent dogs. Consult with a reputable veterinarian to perform thorough physical examinations, including checking for any underlying health conditions or concerns. This step is essential to identify and address any health issues that could be passed down to future generations.

3.2 Genetic Testing:
Consider genetic testing for hereditary diseases specific to the breeds involved in your breeding program. Various DNA tests are available to screen for known genetic disorders, allowing you to make informed breeding decisions.

Collaborate with veterinary geneticists or reputable laboratories to perform these tests and understand the results.

3.3 Breeding Soundness Exams:

Ensure that both potential parent dogs undergo breeding soundness exams. These exams evaluate their reproductive health, including fertility and overall breeding capabilities. Assessing factors like semen quality in males and reproductive health in females will contribute to successful breeding outcomes.

3.4 Pedigree Analysis:

Conduct a thorough analysis of the pedigrees of the potential parent dogs. Study the lineage, considering factors such as breed type, genetic diversity, and the presence of champions or notable dogs within the bloodline. Pedigree analysis can help you identify desirable traits and understand the potential genetic risks associated with specific breeding combinations.

3.5 Understanding Inbreeding and Linebreeding:

Educate yourself about the concepts of inbreeding and linebreeding. While these breeding practices can concentrate desirable traits, they can also increase the risk of inherited health issues. Learn how to calculate and interpret inbreeding coefficients to make informed decisions about maintaining genetic diversity and minimizing potential risks.

3.6 Developing a Breeding Plan:
Based on your health evaluations, genetic testing, and pedigree analysis, develop a comprehensive breeding plan. Consider the goals you have set for your breeding program and select suitable breeding pairs that complement each other in terms of genetics, temperament, and conformation. Incorporate strategies to improve the breed and promote health in future generations.

3.7 Preparing the Breeding Environment:
Create a safe and comfortable breeding environment for the potential parent dogs. Ensure they have ample space, appropriate shelter, and a stress-free atmosphere. Familiarize yourself with the optimal timing for breeding based on the female dog's estrus cycle, and be prepared to provide the necessary support during the breeding process.

3.8 Documentation and Record-Keeping:
Establish a system for meticulous documentation and record-keeping. Maintain detailed records of health evaluations, genetic test results, pedigrees, breeding dates, and any other pertinent information. Accurate record-keeping will assist you in tracking the progress of your breeding program and making informed decisions for future breeding endeavors.

Puppy Love 101

3.9 Responsible Breeding Contracts:
Consider implementing responsible breeding contracts for puppy buyers. These contracts can include clauses related to health guarantees, spay/neuter agreements, and return policies in case the buyer can no longer care for the dog. Responsible breeding contracts help protect the well-being of the puppies you produce and ensure their long-term welfare.

Conclusion:
Preparing for breeding requires a thorough focus on health, genetics, and screening. By conducting health evaluations, genetic testing, pedigree analysis, and breeding soundness exams, you will establish a strong foundation for responsible breeding practices. Developing a breeding plan, preparing the breeding environment, maintaining meticulous records, and implementing responsible breeding contracts will further contribute to the overall success and well-being of your breeding program. Remember, prioritizing health and genetics is essential to producing healthy, happy puppies and making a positive impact on the breed as a whole.

Puppy Love 101

Chapter 4: The Mating Process: From Courtship to Successful Breeding

Introduction:
In this chapter, we'll explore the intricate process of mating dogs, from the initial courtship to achieving successful breeding. Breeding dogs involves understanding their natural behaviours, recognizing signs of readiness for mating, and facilitating the breeding process in a safe and controlled manner. By following these guidelines, you can increase the chances of successful breeding and the subsequent arrival of healthy puppies.

4.1 Understanding Natural Behaviors:
Before proceeding with the mating process, familiarize yourself with the natural behaviors of dogs during mating. Dogs have unique mating rituals, such as sniffing, posturing, and vocalizations. Observing these behaviors will help you identify signs of interest and readiness for mating.

4.2 Timing the Breeding:
Determining the optimal timing for breeding is crucial. Female dogs have a limited fertile period, known as estrus or heat. Monitor the female's behavior and physical signs, such as swelling of the vulva and discharge, to identify when she is in heat. Consult with a veterinarian to confirm the most appropriate timing for successful breeding.

4.3 Preparing the Mating Environment:
Create a suitable and controlled environment for mating. Choose a neutral location where both dogs can comfortably interact. Ensure there are no distractions or potential hazards that may disrupt the mating process. Keep the area secure to prevent any unwanted escapes or interruptions.

4.4 Introducing the Dogs:
Introduce the male and female dogs gradually and under controlled circumstances. Allow them to interact and become familiar with each other's presence. Supervise their interactions to ensure they are comfortable and display positive behaviors. Never force dogs into mating if they show signs of discomfort or aggression.

4.5 Natural Mating:
In natural mating, the male dog mounts the female from behind and achieves penetration. This process occurs naturally when the female is receptive and ready for mating. It is important to allow the dogs to mate naturally and avoid interfering, as their instinctual behaviors are essential for successful breeding.

4.6 Assisted Mating:
In some cases, assisted mating may be required due to size differences, physical limitations, or breeding complications.

Assisted mating involves human intervention to facilitate the mating process. Consult with a veterinarian or an experienced breeder for guidance on the correct techniques and practices for assisted mating, ensuring the safety and comfort of both dogs.

4.7 Post-Mating Care:

After mating, provide a calm and comfortable environment for the female. Rest and minimal physical activity are recommended to increase the chances of successful fertilization. Monitor the female for any signs of discomfort or complications following mating. If necessary, seek veterinary assistance to ensure her well-being.

4.8 Repeat Breedings:

In some cases, multiple breedings may be necessary to increase the chances of successful fertilization. Consult with a veterinarian or an experienced breeder to determine the appropriate frequency and timing of repeat breedings. Avoid excessive breeding attempts, as it may cause stress and discomfort to the female.

4.9 Pregnancy Confirmation:

After the mating process, consult with a veterinarian to confirm pregnancy. This can be done through various methods, such as ultrasound or hormone tests. Early pregnancy confirmation allows for proper care and management during the gestation period.

4.10 Record-Keeping:
Maintain accurate records of the mating process, including dates, times, and any observations made during the mating. Record-keeping is essential for tracking breeding outcomes, estimating due dates, and assisting in future breeding decisions.

Conclusion:
The mating process requires careful observation, understanding, and consideration of the natural behaviours and reproductive cycles of dogs. By recognizing signs of readiness, providing a suitable environment, facilitating natural or assisted mating, and ensuring post-mating care, you can increase the likelihood of successful breeding. Remember to consult with experienced breeders or veterinarians when needed and maintain thorough records of the mating process. With proper attention and care, you'll be on your way to welcoming a litter of healthy and happy puppies.

Chapter 5: Pregnancy and Whelping: Nurturing the Expectant Mother

Introduction:
Congratulations! Your dog is expecting a litter of puppies. This chapter will guide you through the journey of pregnancy and whelping, providing valuable insights on how to support and care for the expectant mother during this special time. By understanding the stages of pregnancy, preparing for whelping, and ensuring proper care, you'll help create a safe and nurturing environment for both the mother and her puppies.

5.1 Confirming Pregnancy:
Consult with a veterinarian to confirm the pregnancy of your dog. This can be done through various methods, such as ultrasound or hormone tests. Knowing the exact stage of pregnancy is important for proper care and management throughout the gestation period.

5.2 Nutritional Needs:
During pregnancy, the expectant mother's nutritional requirements increase. Provide a balanced and high-quality diet that is specifically formulated for pregnant and nursing dogs. Consult with a veterinarian to determine the appropriate type and amount of food to support the health of the mother and the optimal development of the puppies.

5.3 Exercise and Activity:
Moderate exercise is beneficial for the pregnant dog, as it helps maintain muscle tone and overall well-being. However, avoid excessive or strenuous exercise that may cause stress or strain on the mother. Provide regular opportunities for gentle exercise, such as short walks or supervised play sessions.

5.4 Monitoring Health:
Monitor the expectant mother's health closely throughout the pregnancy. Regularly check her body condition, weight, and general well-being. Watch for any signs of discomfort, abnormal behavior, or health issues, and promptly consult with a veterinarian if you have any concerns.

5.5 Nesting Area:
Create a comfortable and secure nesting area for the expectant mother. Set up a whelping box or a designated space that is warm, quiet, and easily accessible. Line the area with clean bedding, ensuring it is soft and comfortable for the mother and her puppies.

5.6 Preparing for Whelping:
Educate yourself about the signs and stages of labor. Familiarize yourself with the typical duration of pregnancy for your dog's breed. As the due date approaches, gather necessary supplies, including clean towels, disinfectants, and a whelping kit. Have emergency contact information for a veterinarian readily available.

5.7 Whelping Process:
During whelping, provide support and monitor the mother closely. Allow her to follow her natural instincts, as she will typically take the lead in the birthing process. Be present to provide assistance if needed, but avoid interfering unnecessarily. Consult with a veterinarian if there are any complications or concerns.

5.8 Post-Whelping Care:
After whelping, ensure the mother and her puppies receive proper care. Allow the mother to bond with her puppies and nurse them regularly. Provide a quiet and stress-free environment for the family. Monitor the puppies' weight gain and overall health, and seek veterinary assistance if any issues arise.

5.9 Lactation and Nutrition:
Support the lactation process by continuing to provide a nutritious diet for the mother. Ensure she has access to clean and fresh water at all times. Consult with a veterinarian if you have any questions or concerns about the mother's nutrition or lactation.

5.10 Emotional Support:
Offer plenty of love, care, and emotional support to the mother throughout the entire process. Spend quality time with her, provide gentle reassurance, and monitor her behavior and emotional well-being.

Puppy Love 101

A calm and nurturing environment will contribute to the overall health and happiness of both the mother and her puppies.

Conclusion:

Pregnancy and whelping are transformative experiences for the expectant mother and a joyous occasion for breeders. By confirming pregnancy, addressing nutritional needs, monitoring health, providing a comfortable nesting area, preparing for whelping, and offering post-whelping care, you can create an environment that supports the mother's well-being and the healthy development of her puppies. Remember to consult with a veterinarian for guidance throughout the process and provide the emotional support and love that the expectant mother deserves.

Puppy Love 101

Chapter 6: Caring for Newborn Puppies: The First Weeks of Life

Introduction:
Welcoming a litter of newborn puppies is an incredibly rewarding experience. In this chapter, we'll explore the essential aspects of caring for newborn puppies during their first weeks of life. From providing a nurturing environment to ensuring their health and development, this guide will help you navigate this critical phase and set the foundation for happy and healthy puppies.

6.1 Creating a Whelping Area:
Designate a warm and clean whelping area for the mother and her puppies. Ensure the space is quiet, free from drafts, and easily accessible. Line the area with soft and clean bedding to provide comfort and warmth. Monitor the temperature to keep it within the appropriate range for newborn puppies.

6.2 Monitoring Health and Vital Signs:
Regularly observe the newborn puppies to monitor their health and vital signs. Check for normal breathing patterns, steady weight gain, and alertness. Be aware of any signs of distress, such as prolonged crying, difficulty nursing, or unusual behaviors. If you notice any concerns, consult with a veterinarian promptly.

6.3 Proper Nutrition and Nursing:
Ensure the mother dog is providing proper nutrition to her puppies through nursing. Monitor the puppies' nursing habits, ensuring they latch onto the mother's nipples and nurse effectively. Watch for signs of adequate milk production, such as satisfied puppies and steady weight gain. If there are any issues with nursing or milk production, seek veterinary advice.

6.4 Maintaining Hygiene:
Maintain a clean and hygienic environment for the newborn puppies. Clean the whelping area regularly, removing any soiled bedding and ensuring a fresh and dry space for the puppies. Gently clean the puppies if necessary, using a warm, damp cloth to wipe away any discharge or debris.

6.5 Socialization and Bonding:
Encourage early socialization and bonding between the puppies and humans. Handle the puppies gently and frequently to promote positive interactions and familiarity with human touch. This helps develop their social skills and prepares them for future interactions and training.

6.6 Monitoring Growth and Development:
Monitor the growth and development of the puppies during their first weeks of life. Keep track of their weight, physical milestones, and behavior patterns.

Consult with a veterinarian for guidance on expected growth rates and any concerns related to the puppies' development.

6.7 Introducing Solid Food:

Around three to four weeks of age, gradually introduce solid food to the puppies. Start with moistened puppy food or a specially formulated puppy gruel. Observe their readiness and appetite for solid food, and adjust the consistency and frequency of feedings accordingly.

6.8 Preventing Health Issues:

Take preventative measures to ensure the health of the newborn puppies. Keep the whelping area clean, discourage excessive handling by strangers, and restrict access to prevent exposure to infectious diseases. Follow a deworming schedule recommended by a veterinarian to prevent parasites.

6.9 Vaccinations and Veterinary Care:

Consult with a veterinarian to establish a vaccination schedule for the puppies. Vaccinations help protect them against common diseases. Schedule regular veterinary check-ups to monitor the puppies' health and address any concerns or issues that may arise.

6.10 Emotional Support and Enrichment:

Provide emotional support and enriching experiences for the puppies. Spend time with them daily, gently playing and interacting to foster their mental and emotional development. Introduce age-appropriate toys and stimuli to stimulate their senses and promote cognitive growth.

Puppy Love 101

Conclusion:
The first weeks of life are crucial for the development and well-being of newborn puppies. By creating a comfortable and clean whelping area, monitoring their health and vital signs, ensuring proper nutrition and nursing, maintaining hygiene, promoting socialization and bonding, monitoring growth and development, introducing solid food, preventing health issues, scheduling veterinary care, and providing emotional support and enrichment, you'll lay the groundwork for healthy and well-adjusted puppies. Enjoy this precious time with the puppies and seek veterinary guidance whenever needed to ensure their optimal health and development.

Puppy Love 101

Chapter 7: Early Puppy Development: Socialization, Training, and Bonding

Introduction:
The early stages of a puppy's life are critical for its socialization, training, and bonding with humans and other animals. This chapter will guide you through the important aspects of early puppy development, providing valuable insights on how to foster their social skills, implement basic training, and strengthen the bond between you and your furry friend.

7.1 Socialization:
Early socialization is key to a puppy's overall development. Expose your puppy to a variety of experiences, people, animals, and environments in a safe and controlled manner. Introduce them to different sights, sounds, and textures to help build their confidence and reduce the likelihood of fear or anxiety later in life.

7.2 Gentle Handling and Positive Experiences:
Handle your puppy gently and positively from an early age. Encourage calm and positive interactions by using soft voices, gentle touches, and rewards. This will help build trust and a positive association with the human touch, making future grooming, vet visits, and handling easier.

Puppy Love 101

7.3 Puppy Classes and Socialization Opportunities:
Enroll your puppy in puppy classes or socialization groups. These provide opportunities for your puppy to interact with other dogs and people in a controlled and supervised environment. Such experiences promote proper social behavior, improve communication skills, and strengthen their ability to adapt to new situations.

7.4 Basic Training:
Begin basic training exercises as early as possible. Teach your puppy simple commands such as "sit," "stay," and "come." Use positive reinforcement techniques, such as treats and praise, to encourage desired behaviors. Consistency, patience, and short training sessions will help your puppy grasp these foundational commands.

7.5 House Training:
Start house training your puppy as soon as they come home. Establish a routine for regular bathroom breaks and reward your puppy for eliminating in the appropriate area. Be consistent with the schedule and provide ample opportunities for your puppy to succeed. Accidents may happen, but with time and consistent training, your puppy will learn where to relieve themselves.

7.6 Chew Toy Training:
Puppies have a natural urge to chew, which is important for teething and jaw development.

Puppy Love 101

Provide a variety of appropriate chew toys and encourage your puppy to chew on them rather than household items. Redirect their attention to the toys and praise them when they engage in appropriate chewing behavior.

7.7 Leash Training:

Introduce your puppy to leash walking gradually. Start by allowing them to become accustomed to wearing a collar or harness. Then, attach a lightweight leash and let them walk around indoors or in a secure area. Reward them for walking calmly beside you. Over time, increase the duration and complexity of your walks while reinforcing good leash manners.

7.8 Socializing with Other Animals:

Expose your puppy to friendly and well-socialized dogs, cats, and other animals. Monitor their interactions and ensure they are positive and controlled. These experiences will help your puppy develop proper social skills and become comfortable around different species.

7.9 Bonding and Quality Time:

Spend dedicated quality time with your puppy every day. Engage in activities such as playtime, grooming sessions, and gentle petting. Use this time to strengthen your bond and build trust. The more positive experiences you share, the deeper the bond between you and your puppy will grow.

Puppy Love 101

7.10 Patience and Consistency:
Remember that each puppy develops at their own pace.
Be patient and understanding during the training and
socialization process. Consistency is key, so maintain a
predictable routine and reinforce desired behaviors
consistently. Celebrate small victories and focus on
positive progress.
Conclusion:
Early puppy development sets the foundation for their
future behavior and well-being. By prioritizing
socialization, gentle handling, positive experiences,
basic training, house training, chew toy training, leash
training, socializing with other animals, bonding, and
quality time, you'll help your puppy grow into a
confident, well-adjusted, and obedient companion. Be
patient, consistent, and enjoy the journey of watching
your puppy flourish into a wonderful adult dog with a
strong bond to you.

Puppy Love 101

Chapter 8: Nutritional Needs: Feeding the Growing Puppies and Their Mother

Introduction:
Proper nutrition is essential for the healthy growth and development of both puppies and their mother. In this chapter, we'll explore the nutritional needs of growing puppies and provide guidance on feeding practices to support their overall well-being. Additionally, we'll discuss the importance of a balanced diet for the mother during the lactation period. By understanding their specific dietary requirements, you can ensure optimal nutrition for the entire family.

8.1 Consult with a Veterinarian:
Consult with a veterinarian to determine the most appropriate diet for your puppies and their mother. They can assess the specific needs of your breed, the number of puppies, and any individual health considerations. A veterinarian will provide valuable guidance on feeding practices and help you select high-quality, commercial puppy food or provide a recipe for a balanced homemade diet.

8.2 Feeding the Mother Dog:
During the lactation period, the mother dog's nutritional needs increase significantly. Provide her with a high-quality dog food formulated for nursing mothers.

This food should be nutritionally dense, providing ample protein, vitamins, minerals, and calories to support milk production and maintain her overall health. Ensure the mother has access to fresh water at all times.

8.3 Puppy Food Transition:

Around the age of three to four weeks, gradually introduce solid food to the puppies while continuing to provide nursing from the mother. Begin with moistened puppy food or a specially formulated puppy gruel. Monitor the puppies' readiness for solid food and adjust the consistency and frequency of feedings accordingly.

8.4 High-Quality Puppy Food:

Select a high-quality commercial puppy food that is specifically formulated to meet the nutritional needs of growing puppies. Look for a brand that has undergone rigorous testing and meets the Association of American Feed Control Officials (AAFCO) standards. These foods are balanced to provide the necessary nutrients for proper growth and development.

8.5 Scheduled Feeding:

Establish a regular feeding schedule for the puppies. Divide their daily food allowance into several small meals throughout the day to support their digestion and prevent overeating. Avoid free-feeding, as it can lead to obesity and poor eating habits.

8.6 Gradual Weaning Process:
Gradually wean the puppies from their mother's milk by reducing the nursing sessions over time. Encourage them to rely more on solid food for their nutritional needs. Monitor their weight and overall health during the weaning process to ensure a smooth transition.

8.7 Monitoring Weight and Growth:
Regularly monitor the puppies' weight and growth to ensure they are developing appropriately. Weigh them weekly to track their progress. A healthy weight gain indicates proper nutrition, while sudden weight loss or poor growth may require veterinary attention.

8.8 Avoid Overfeeding:
While it is important to provide proper nutrition, avoid overfeeding the puppies. Excessive weight gain can lead to health problems and developmental issues. Follow the feeding guidelines provided by your veterinarian or the puppy food manufacturer, and adjust portion sizes based on the puppies' growth and development.

8.9 Fresh Water Availability:
Ensure the puppies have access to clean and fresh water at all times, especially after they start consuming solid food. Monitor their water intake and refill their water bowl regularly. Adequate hydration is crucial for their overall health and digestion.

Puppy Love 101

8.10 Transition to Adult Food:
Around the age of six to twelve months, depending on the breed, transition the puppies to high-quality, age-appropriate adult dog food. Consult with a veterinarian for guidance on the timing and specific nutritional requirements for your breed.
Conclusion:
Proper nutrition is vital for the healthy growth and development of puppies and their mother. Consult with a veterinarian to determine the most appropriate diet and feeding practices for your specific situation. Provide high-quality puppy food, establish a feeding schedule, monitor weight and growth, avoid overfeeding, ensure fresh water availability, and plan for a gradual transition to adult food. By prioritizing their nutritional needs, you'll lay the foundation for a healthy and vibrant future for both the puppies and their mother.

Puppy Love 101

Chapter 9: Health and Veterinary Care: Preventive Measures and Regular Checkups

Introduction:
Ensuring the health and well-being of your dogs is essential for their quality of life. In this chapter, we'll explore the importance of preventive measures and regular veterinary care in maintaining the overall health of your dogs. From vaccinations to routine checkups, we'll cover key aspects of proactive healthcare that will help keep your furry companions happy and thriving.

9.1 Vaccinations:
Vaccinations play a vital role in preventing infectious diseases in dogs. Consult with a veterinarian to establish a vaccination schedule tailored to your dogs' specific needs. Vaccinations typically protect against diseases such as distemper, parvovirus, hepatitis, and rabies. Stay up to date with recommended booster shots to ensure continuous protection.

9.2 Parasite Prevention:
Implement a comprehensive parasite prevention program to protect your dogs from fleas, ticks, heartworms, and intestinal parasites. Use veterinary-recommended products such as flea and tick preventatives, heartworm preventatives, and regular deworming treatments.

Puppy Love 101

Regularly inspect your dogs for signs of parasites and consult with a veterinarian if you suspect an infestation.

9.3 Dental Care:

Maintaining good oral hygiene is essential for your dogs' overall health. Brush their teeth regularly using a pet-specific toothbrush and toothpaste. Additionally, provide appropriate chew toys and dental treats to help reduce tartar buildup. Schedule regular dental checkups and cleanings with a veterinarian to address any potential dental issues.

9.4 Regular Checkups:

Schedule regular checkups with a veterinarian to monitor your dogs' overall health and address any concerns. These routine visits allow the veterinarian to perform thorough physical examinations, assess vital signs, and screen for any underlying health issues. Regular checkups enable early detection and intervention, leading to better health outcomes.

9.5 Nutritional Guidance:

Consult with a veterinarian to ensure your dogs are receiving a balanced and appropriate diet for their specific needs. Discuss their nutritional requirements, portion sizes, and feeding schedules. Veterinary guidance will help you select high-quality commercial dog food or develop a well-balanced homemade diet.

9.6 Exercise and Weight Management:
Regular exercise is crucial for your dogs' physical and mental well-being. Provide opportunities for daily physical activity through walks, playtime, and interactive games. Monitor their weight and body condition regularly to ensure they maintain a healthy weight. Consult with a veterinarian for guidance on exercise routines and weight management strategies.

9.7 Senior Dog Care:
As your dogs age, their healthcare needs may change. Schedule more frequent veterinary checkups for senior dogs to monitor for age-related conditions such as arthritis, cognitive decline, and dental issues. Work with your veterinarian to develop a tailored care plan that addresses the specific needs of your senior dogs.

9.8 Grooming and Skin Care:
Regular grooming is important for maintaining your dogs' skin and coat health. Brush their fur regularly, check for any signs of skin issues or abnormalities, and provide appropriate grooming, such as bathing and trimming nails. Consult with a veterinarian if you notice any skin problems or changes in coat quality.

9.9 Behavior and Training:
Address any behavioral concerns or training needs promptly. Consult with a veterinarian or a professional dog trainer to address issues such as aggression, anxiety, or inappropriate behaviors.

Puppy Love 101

Early intervention and positive reinforcement training methods can help improve your dogs' behavior and overall well-being.

9.10 Emergency Preparedness:

Prepare for potential emergencies by having a first aid kit and emergency contact numbers readily available. Familiarize yourself with basic first aid procedures and know when to seek immediate veterinary care. Being prepared ensures prompt and appropriate action in case of injuries or sudden illness.

Conclusion:

Taking proactive measures and prioritizing regular veterinary care are essential for maintaining your dogs' health and well-being. Vaccinations, parasite prevention, dental care, regular checkups, proper nutrition, exercise, weight management, grooming, addressing behavioral concerns, and emergency preparedness are all crucial aspects of responsible healthcare. By making preventive measures and regular veterinary care a priority, you'll be able to provide your dogs with the best possible chance at a long, healthy, and happy life.

Puppy Love 101

Chapter 10: Finding Loving Homes: Responsible Placement and Adoption Procedures

Introduction:
Finding loving and suitable homes for your puppies is a crucial responsibility as a breeder. In this chapter, we'll discuss the importance of responsible placement and adoption procedures. From screening potential adopters to ensuring a smooth transition for the puppies, we'll explore the steps you can take to find the best possible homes for your puppies and promote responsible pet ownership.

10.1 Screening Potential Adopters:
Thoroughly screen potential adopters to ensure they are prepared to provide a loving and suitable home for your puppies. Ask questions about their lifestyle, experience with dogs, family dynamics, and their expectations of owning a dog. Consider conducting home visits or virtual interviews to assess their living environment and suitability.

10.2 Evaluating Compatibility:
Evaluate the compatibility between the potential adopters and the specific needs of the puppies. Consider factors such as activity levels, living arrangements, and the adopters' ability to meet the puppies' specific requirements. Aim to match each puppy with an adopter who can provide an environment that aligns with their temperament and energy level.

10.3 Educating Adopters:

Educate potential adopters about responsible pet ownership, the breed characteristics, and the responsibilities involved in caring for a dog. Provide information on grooming, exercise requirements, training, socialization, and the importance of regular veterinary care. Ensure that potential adopters understand the commitment they are making.

10.4 Adoption Contracts:

Develop clear and comprehensive adoption contracts that outline the responsibilities of both the adopters and the breeder. Include clauses related to spaying/neutering, responsible breeding practices, return policies, and any health guarantees or agreements. These contracts help protect the well-being of the puppies and ensure they are placed in appropriate homes.

10.5 Transition and Support:

Facilitate a smooth transition for the puppies from your care to their new homes. Provide information on the puppies' routines, diet, and any specific needs or preferences. Offer support and guidance to adopters during the initial adjustment period and be available to answer any questions or concerns they may have.

10.6 Follow-Up and Continued Support:

Follow up with adopters after the puppies have settled into their new homes.

Puppy Love 101

Inquire about their progress, address any issues that may arise, and offer continued support. Maintain open lines of communication to ensure the well-being of the puppies and provide guidance throughout their lives.

10.7 Responsible Advertising:

Advertise responsibly when seeking potential adopters. Use reputable platforms and channels that attract individuals who are genuinely interested in providing a loving home for a dog. Avoid misleading or exaggerated claims and provide accurate information about the breed, the puppies, and the adoption process.

10.8 Rehoming and Rescue Organizations:

Consider partnering with rehoming or rescue organizations if you encounter challenges finding suitable homes for your puppies. These organizations have experience in evaluating potential adopters and may have a wider network of potential homes available. Collaboration with reputable organizations can help ensure the long-term well-being of the puppies.

10.9 Spaying/Neutering Requirements:

Include spaying or neutering requirements in your adoption contracts to prevent unwanted litters and promote responsible pet ownership. Discuss the importance of this procedure with adopters and, if necessary, provide guidance on reputable veterinarians who can perform the procedure.

Puppy Love 101

10.10 Breed-Specific Rescue Referrals:
If adopters are unable to keep the puppy in the future, provide information on breed-specific rescue organizations that can assist with rehoming. These organizations specialize in placing dogs of specific breeds and can help ensure the puppies find suitable homes even if circumstances change.
Conclusion:
Finding loving and responsible homes for your puppies is a critical aspect of being a breeder. By screening potential adopters, evaluating compatibility, educating adopters, implementing clear adoption contracts, facilitating a smooth transition, offering ongoing support, advertising responsibly, and considering partnerships with rehoming or rescue organizations, you can promote responsible pet ownership and ensure the long-term well-being of the puppies. By taking these steps, you'll contribute to building a community of loving and responsible dog owners who will provide a lifetime of care and love for your puppies.

Puppy Love 101

Thank you for your interest in "Puppy Love 101: A Beginner's Guide to Dog Breeding." We hope this guide has provided you with valuable insights and practical advice to embark on your journey as a responsible dog breeder. Remember, the world of dog breeding is a labor of love, and it requires dedication, knowledge, and a deep commitment to the well-being of these incredible creatures. By applying the principles and guidelines outlined in this guide, you can contribute to the betterment of the canine community and create a positive impact on the lives of dogs and their owners. May your breeding endeavors be filled with joy, success, and an abundance of puppy love. Good luck on your exciting journey, and may you continue to experience the immeasurable rewards that come from fostering the beautiful bond between dogs and humans.

Puppy Love 101